Searchlight
BOOKS™

Getting into Government

Exploring

Voting and Elections

Jennifer Joline Anderson

Lerner Publications ◆ Minneapolis

This book is dedicated to my children, Ruby
and Henry, and to all kids who will vote for
the leaders of the future.

Lerner Publications Company
An imprint of Lerner Publishing Group, Inc.
241 First Avenue North
Minneapolis, MN 55401 USA

For reading levels and more information, look up this title
at www.lernerbooks.com.

Library of Congress Cataloging-in-Publication Data

Names: Anderson, Jennifer Joline, author.
Title: Exploring voting and elections / by Jennifer Joline Anderson.
Description: Minneapolis : Lerner Publications, 2020. | Series: Searchlight books. Getting
    into government | Includes bibliographical references and index. | Audience: Age
    8–11. | Audience: Grade 4 to 6.
Identifiers: LCCN 2018044384 (print) | LCCN 2018046056 (ebook) |
    ISBN 9781541556744 (eb pdf) | ISBN 9781541555846 (lb : alk. paper)
Subjects: LCSH: Voting—United States—Juvenile literature. | Elections—United States—
    Juvenile literature. | Presidents—United States—Election—Juvenile literature.
Classification: LCC JK1978 (ebook) | LCC JK1978 .A196 2020 (print) | DDC 324.973—dc23

LC record available at https://lccn.loc.gov/2018044384

Manufactured in the United States of America
1-46039-43362-4/4/2019

Contents

Chapter 1

ELECTION DAY

Tuesday, November 8, 2016, was an exciting day. Voters in the United States were ready to choose a new president. The top candidates were Hillary Clinton and Donald Trump. Clinton was a politician. She had worked in government for years. Trump was a famous business owner. He had not worked in politics before, but many people liked his ideas.

Before an election, candidates participate in a series of debates to discuss their ideas and plans.

TRUMP AND HIS SUPPORTERS CELEBRATED TRUMP'S VICTORY AT PARTIES AROUND THE COUNTRY.

A lot of political reporters predicted that Clinton would win. Many voters went to bed on the night of the election believing that Clinton would be the next president. As the votes were counted later that evening, there was a big surprise. Trump had beat Clinton. He was elected the forty-fifth president of the United States.

The People Decide

People in the United States vote on Election Day. Election Day is always on a Tuesday in early November. People vote for the president every four years. They vote for other politicians every two, four, or six years. Every Election Day is different, but the results are always exciting. Nobody can know who will win until the election is finished. It is up to the people who come out to vote.

People who vote on Election Day often get a sticker that says "I Voted."

Chapter 2

WHY WE VOTE

The United States is a democracy. That means the government is run by the people. In US elections, the people vote for the leaders who will represent them. Voting gives people power in their government. Elected leaders know they must do what is best for the people. If they do not do their job well, people might not vote for them in the next election.

Voters try to pick leaders who will make fair laws for the country.

Whom Do We Vote For?

The national government in the United States has three branches, or parts. They are the legislative branch, the judicial branch, and the executive branch. The president is the leader of the executive branch, which carries out laws. Congress is the legislative branch, which makes the laws. People vote to choose the members of Congress who will represent their own state and district in national government.

After a bill passes in Congress, the president signs it into law.

Government Affects You

Government leaders have the power to make laws that people want. In the 1960s and 1970s, voters were worried about pollution. Congress responded by passing the Clean Air Act and the Clean Water Act. The goal of these laws was to stop companies from polluting the air we breathe and the water we drink.

The Clean Air Act and Clean Water Act forced some companies to do business in ways that better protected the environment.

A sheriff speaks during a news conference. People vote for sheriffs in local elections.

Electing State and Local Leaders

People also vote for local leaders in elections. They vote for the leader of the state government. This person is called the governor. States have their own group of lawmakers. They are state senators and state representatives.

Elections also help decide the leaders of a city or town government. There are many other types of elected leaders. For example, people can vote for members of the school board or park board. These leaders help make decisions about schools and parks.

Who Can Vote?

American citizens must be eighteen years of age or older to vote. People vote in the area where they live. They need to register, or sign up, to vote. To do this, they must prove where they live. In some states, voters must also show identification when they go to vote to show who they are.

Some states allow voters to register on the day of the election.

That's a Fact!

Only white men who owned property could vote in the earliest US elections. In 1870, the Fifteenth Amendment to the US Constitution stated that African American men had the right to vote. Women won the right to vote in 1920. Other groups had to fight for their right to vote too. In 1965, a law called the Voting Rights Act made it illegal to stop other people from voting.

Women protested to win the right to vote.

Chapter 3

THE ELECTION PROCESS

Candidates work hard to get people to vote for them. They hold meetings and give speeches. They may also hand out flyers, run ads on television, post messages on social media websites, or send emails to voters. They tell voters what they plan to do if elected.

People who like a candidate might help the candidate. The supporters also work hard to convince other people to vote for their candidate.

Many candidates go out to talk to members of their community in person.

Debates bring candidates together so people watching can decide whom they want to vote for.

Candidates often participate in debates. In a debate, the candidates talk about important issues. They explain how they would solve problems in the nation and in their community. Candidates might have different views about the problems. People watching can decide which candidate they agree with.

Join the Party!

Most candidates are members of a political party. Political parties are made up of people who often have the same ideas and goals for the government. The party helps support candidates in elections. The two largest parties in the United States are the Democratic Party and the Republican Party. Smaller parties are called third parties. Some candidates do not belong to any party. They are independent candidates.

The Green Party is one of the bigger third parties.

Government Affects You

People pay taxes to the government. The government uses this money to pay for things the community needs. When the government needs more money to pay for things, people might vote on whether they want to pay more money in taxes.

For example, if your school needed money to build a gym, people in the community might vote yes or no on raising taxes. Voting might make a difference in what your school can do.

Public schools use money from taxes to build gyms, buy books, and pay teachers.

Primary Elections

Many candidates might want to be elected to serve in the government. Smaller elections, called primary elections, are held earlier to shorten the list of candidates. People vote in these primary elections to decide which candidates they like best from each political party. Candidates hope to win enough votes in the primary elections to run in the final election in November.

Fewer people tend to vote in primary elections than in final elections.

Hillary Clinton gives a speech at the Democratic National Convention.

After people vote in primary elections, political parties decide which candidates they plan to support. Usually, parties support the candidates that won in the primary elections. These decisions are announced at conventions. The two biggest conventions for a presidential election are the Republican National Convention and the Democratic National Convention. Supporters gather at conventions to hear which candidates they might vote for in November.

Election Day

On Election Day, people go to polling places. Members of a community can vote there. A polling place may be in a public building such as a school or fire station. People working at the polling place get it ready for voters. The workers check that each voter is voting in the right place.

Some poll workers are called election judges.

Each voter gets a ballot. A ballot may be a sheet of paper, a card, or an electronic form with a list of the candidates. Voters show which candidates they want to vote for by marking their names on the ballot in private. They do not see other people's ballots. In some states, voters can send their ballot in the mail before Election Day.

Once a person has voted, the ballot is placed in a safe place until it is time to count the votes.

Counting the Votes

At the end of the day, the votes from every polling place are counted. Usually the winners are announced on election night. If an election is very close, it may take longer to count the votes. This happened in 2000, when candidates Al Gore and George W. Bush were running for president. The election was so close that votes had to be recounted many times before the winner was announced more than a month after the election.

George W. Bush was announced the winner of the 2000 presidential election after a close race.

The Electoral College

In many elections, a candidate wins by getting the most votes. This is the popular vote.

A presidential election is different. People vote on Election Day to pick which candidate they like as president. Then the Electoral College, a smaller group of people, votes for a president.

TRUMP WAS VOTED INTO OFFICE
BY THE ELECTORAL COLLEGE.

Members of the Electoral College met on December 19, 2016, to cast their votes for the 2016 presidential election.

The Electoral College has electors in each state. Electors vote in December. The number of electors in each state depends on the number of people who live in that state. Electors are supposed to vote for the candidate who wins the most votes in their community. To win the election, the candidate must win a majority of the votes cast by the Electoral College.

That's a Fact!

A president can win the most votes in the popular vote and still lose the election. This has happened five times in US history: in 1824, in 1876, in 1888, in 2000, and in 2016. Each time, the winner of the election actually got fewer votes overall but was able to win more votes in the Electoral College. For example, in 2016, Hillary Clinton won the popular vote, but Trump had more electoral votes.

Clinton gave a speech after she found out that she lost the 2016 presidential election to Trump.

Chapter 4

GET INVOLVED

During election years, some schools hold their own elections. Students can cast their own votes at school. These votes are not counted officially, but students get to practice voting. They may compare the results at their own school to the results of the official election.

Students practice their voting skills before they can cast a ballot in an official national election.

Running for student government is a great way to practice leadership skills.

Voting in School

Many schools have a student government. The student government might help organize special events. They can help make changes that students want to see at school. Often students get to vote on candidates for their student government.

There also may be other votes at school. For example, students may vote on what type of animal to get for a class pet.

A group might get together and hold signs or chant messages for leaders to hear.

Other Ways to Get Involved

Even if they can't vote, students can get involved in an election. Students can encourage adults to vote. They can support a candidate for office by making signs or talking to people about issues. Students can also get together as a group to show support for an important issue.

A good way to become involved in government is to take part in issues that affect your community. Neighborhoods often have organizations to make the community cleaner and safer. Volunteering for a community organization is a good way to learn how politics works. Even if you can't vote, you can do a lot to help your community and nation.

It's never too soon to get involved.

Who's Right?

Some people think teens under eighteen should be able to vote. Some do not.

Some argue that kids won't know enough to vote. Kids in school are still learning about how government works. People are worried kids may not understand issues well enough to make a good decision.

But if kids voted, politicians might pay more attention to issues that impact younger people, such as education and school safety. They might listen to kids and hear new ideas.

Who is right? Are children under eighteen too young to vote? Why or why not?

Glossary

ballot: a card, sheet of paper, or electronic form used to cast votes in an election

candidate: a person who runs in an election

district: an area or section of a city or nation

Electoral College: a group of people who cast the deciding votes for the US president

political party: a group of people who share similar ideas and goals for government

politician: a person who takes an active part in politics or in government

polling place: the place where people go to cast their votes

predict: to guess the outcome of something in advance based on observations and experience

primary election: an election held before the final election to narrow down the list of candidates

third party: a political party other than the two largest parties in the United States

Learn More about Voting and Elections

Books

Beckett, Leslie. *Does Voting Matter?* New York: KidHaven, 2018. Read this book to learn why every person's vote matters.

Conley, Kate. *Our Elected Leaders.* Minneapolis: Abdo, 2017. Learn more about the election process, and explore the types of powers that rest with leaders of the executive, legislative, and judicial branches.

Krasner, Barbara. *Exploring the Executive Branch.* Minneapolis: Lerner Publications, 2020. Explore the role of the executive branch, including the president, in the US government.

Websites

Ducksters: How Voting Works
https://www.ducksters.com/history/us_government_voting.php
Dive into the voting process, and learn how and why things work the way they do.

Library of Congress: Elections . . . the American Way
http://www.loc.gov/teachers/classroommaterials/presentationsandactivities/presentations/elections/index.html
Visit this page to see photos and real-life documents that teach about the history of elections in the United States.

PBS Kids: You Choose
http://pbskids.org/youchoose
Check out this site for facts and activities related to the United States' most recent presidential election.

Index

Photo Acknowledgments

Image credits: Brooks Kraft/Getty Images, p. 4; Neilson Barnard/WireImage/Getty Images, p. 5; PhilipR/Shutterstock.com, p. 6; Jason Kolenda/Shutterstock.com, p. 6; Rhona Wise/AFP/Getty Images, p. 7; Mandel Ngan/AFP/Getty Images, p. 8; JoyceMarrero/Getty Images, p. 9; Mark Rightmire/Orange County Register/Getty Images, p. 10; John Moore/Getty Images, p. 11; Library of Congress, p. 12; Jessica Rinaldi/The Boston Globe/Getty Images, p. 13; Chris O'Meara/Getty Imag es, p. 14; Son Emmert/AFP/Getty Images, p. 15; ultramarinfoto/Getty Images, p. 16; Matthew Hatcher/SOPA Images/LightRocket/Getty Images, p. 17; Tom Williams/CQ Roll Call/Getty Images, p. 18; Lewis Geyer/Getty Images, p. 19; Atilgan Ozdil/Anadolu Agency/Getty Images, p. 20; Chris Hondros/Getty Images, p. 21; Chip Somodevilla/Getty Images, p. 22; Sarah Rice/Stringer/Getty Images, p. 23; Matt McClain/The Washington Post/Getty Images, p. 24; dolgachov/Getty Images, p. 25; Jupiterimages/Getty Images, p. 26; Win McNamee/Getty Images, p. 27.

Cover: Hero Images/Getty Images.

Main body text set in Adrianna Regular. Typeface provided by Chank.